ALWAYS HAVE TO ENTER THE ROOM BY
ANNOUNCING YOUR LAST NAME

~OR~

ALWAYS HAVE TO DO CARTWHEELS OUT?

DISCOVER A PIRATE TREASURE CHEST

~OR~

DISCOVER A LIVING DINOSAUR?

WOULD YOU RATHER...

KNOW THE ENDING OF EVERY MOVIE BEFORE YOU WATCH IT

~OR~

NOT BE ABLE TO WATCH ANY NEW MOVIE UNTIL IT'S BEEN OUT FOR A YEAR?

BE ABLE TO HOLD YOUR BREATH AS LONG AS A SEAL

~OR~

JUMP AS FAR AS A KANGAROO?

WOULD YOU RATHER...

HAVE ONE EYE ON YOUR FOREHEAD

~OR~

TWO NOSES?

GO TO THE DOCTOR

~OR~

TO THE DENTIST?

WOULD YOU RATHER...

HAVE EDIBLE NOODLE HAIR THAT REGROWS EVERY NIGHT

~OR~

SWEAT SUGAR SYRUP?

BE ABLE TO CHOOSE YOUR AGE ONCE

~OR~

STAY THE AGE YOU ARE NOW FOR ANOTHER 3 YEARS?

WOULD YOU RATHER...

EAT KALE-FLAVORED ICE CREAM

~OR~

MEAT-FLAVORED CANDY?

BE ABLE TO SURVIVE FALLS FROM ANY HEIGHT

~OR~

HAVE A BULLETPROOF SKIN?

LOSE THE ABILITY TO READ

~OR~

LOSE THE ABILITY TO LAUGH?

GO TO ANOTHER PLANET TO START A COLONY

~OR~

BE THE LEADER OF A SMALL COUNTRY HERE ON EARTH?

WOULD YOU RATHER....

KNOW WHAT OTHER PEOPLE THINK

~OR~

KNOW EVERY OUTCOME OF YOUR EVERY CHOICE?

BE ABLE TO SEE THINGS THAT ARE FAR AWAY, LIKE A TELESCOPE

~OR~

BE ABLE TO SEE THINGS VERY CLOSE UP, LIKE A MICROSCOPE?

BE COVERED IN HAIR HEAD TO TOE

~OR~

BE COMPLETELY HAIRLESS?

HAVE TO WEAR A SUPERMAN CAPE EVERY DAY

~OR~

A BATMAN MASK EVERY DAY?

WOULD YOU RATHER...

HAVE TO EAT SOUP WITH A FORK

~OR~

EAT SPAGHETTI WITH A SPOON?

SLEEP IN A DOGHOUSE

~OR~

LET ALL THE STRAY DOGS FROM YOUR
NEIGHBORHOOD SLEEP IN YOUR HOUSE?

BE A CAPTAIN OF THE FOOTBALL TEAM

~OR~

A PIRATE CAPTAIN?

BE FANTASTIC AT FLYING A PLANE

~OR~

AMAZING AT DRIVING A MONSTER TRUCK?

WOULD YOU RATHER...

NEVER HAVE TO TAKE ANOTHER TEST OR EXAM

~OR~

NEVER GET SICK EVER AGAIN?

SOUND LIKE A HYENA

~OR~

LIKE A GOAT WHEN YOU LAUGH?

GO SURFING DURING WINTER

~OR~

GO SKIING DURING SUMMER?

RELIVE THE SAME DAY OVER AND OVER AGAIN FOR TWO YEARS

~OR~

TAKE 3 YEARS OFF YOUR LIFE?

DRINK YOUR FOOD FROM A BABY BOTTLE

~OR~

WEAR VISIBLE DIAPERS?

NOT BE ABLE TO WASH YOUR HANDS FOR A MONTH

~OR~

YOUR HAIR FOR A MONTH?

BE RICH AND GREEDY

~OR~

POOR BUT GENEROUS?

LIVE IN A MUSEUM

~OR~

LIVE IN A THEME PARK?

WOULD YOU RATH-K...

ALWAYS FORGET WHO YOU ARE

~OR~

ALWAYS FORGET WHO EVERYONE ELSE IS?

HAVE LIVED IN THE 1860S

~OR~

IN THE 1960S?

WOULD YOU RATHER...

SWITCH HEADS WITH THE PERSON ON YOUR LEFT

~OR~

THE PERSON ON YOUR RIGHT?

WIN AN OSCAR

~OR~

A NOBEL PRIZE?

WOULD YOU RATHER...

WEAR SOMEONE'S UNDERWEAR

~OR~

USE SOMEONE'S TOOTHBRUSH?

NEVER HAVE BREAKFAST

~OR~

NEVER HAVE DINNER?

WOULD YOU RATHER...

HAVE EYELASHES THAT NEVER STOP GROWING

~OR~

HAIR THAT NEVER GROW BACK AFTER BEING CUT?

BE SO AFRAID OF HEIGHTS THAT YOU CAN'T EVEN STAND ON A STOOL

~OR~

BE SO AFRAID OF THE SUN THAT YOU CAN ONLY LEAVE YOUR HOUSE ON A CLOUDY DAY?

WOULD YOU RATHER...

HAVE TO SAY ALL YOUR SENTENCES BACKWARDS

~OR~

HAVE TO COMMUNICATE VIA SIGN LANGUAGE?

SLEEP STANDING UP

~OR~

WALK SIDEWAYS LIKE A CRAB?

WOULD YOU RATHER...

ALWAYS BE ABLE TO LIE WITHOUT BEING CAUGHT

~OR~

BE ABLE TO TELL WHEN SOMEONE IS LYING?

LOOK YOUNG AND FEEL OLD

~OR~

LOOK OLD BUT FEEL YOUNG?

WOULD YOU RATHER...

TRAVEL BACK IN TIME TO MEET YOUR ANCESTORS

~OR~

TRAVEL TO THE FUTURE TO MEET YOUR GREAT GRANDCHILDREN?

ALWAYS HAVE MISMATCHED SHOES

~OR~

ALWAYS WEAR YOUR PANTS BACKWARDS?

WOULD YOU RATHER...

MEET YOUR FAVORITE COMIC-BOOK CHARACTER

~OR~

YOUR FAVORITE VIDEO GAME CHARACTER?

BE THE STRONGEST PERSON IN THE WORLD

~OR~

THE SMARTEST PERSON IN THE WORLD?

WOULD YOU RATHER....

FIND FIVE DOLLARS ON THE GROUND

~OR~

A PENNY DOUBLED EVERY DAY FOR 15 DAYS?

FORGET YOUR OWN NAME EVERY TIME IT RAINS

~OR~

NEVER BE ABLE TO REMEMBER WHERE YOU LIVE
EVERY TIME IT SNOWS?

HAVE THE LEGS OF A DOG

~OR~

THE HEAD OF A CAT?

GO BALD TOMORROW

~OR~

LOSE ONE TOOTH EACH MONTH?

HANG OUT WITH WINNIE-THE-POOH

~OR~

HANG OUT WITH BALOO FROM THE JUNGLE BOOK?

BE AN UNKNOWN SUPERHERO

~OR~

A FAMOUS VILLAIN?

WOULD YOU RATHER...

HAVE A PERMANENT PIMPLE ON YOUR NOSE

~OR~

HAVE A PERMANENT BAD HAIRCUT?

NEVER BE ABLE TO LEAVE YOUR HOUSE

~OR~

ONLY BE ABLE TO BE IN THE HOUSE FOR TEN MINUTES EVERY DAY?

WOULD YOU RATHER...

HAVE YOUR INDEX FINGER REPLACED WITH YOUR BIG TOE

~OR~

HAVE YOUR PINKY REPLACED WITH YOUR THUMB?

BARK LIKE A DOG WHEN YOU FEEL THREATENED

~OR~

SCREAM LIKE A GOAT?

WOULD YOU RATHER...

NEVER BE ABLE TO WATCH YOUTUBE AGAIN

~OR~

NEVER BE ABLE TO PLAY VIDEO GAMES AGAIN?

ALWAYS BE ONE HOUR EARLY

~OR~

ALWAYS BE FIFTEEN MINUTES LATE?

LIVE IN ONE HOUSE FOR YOUR WHOLE LIFE

~OR~

MOVE TO A DIFFERENT HOUSE EVERY WEEK?

BE ABLE TO INVENT A NEW HOLIDAY

~OR~

INVENT A NEW SPORT OR RECREATIONAL GAME?

WOULD YOU RATHER...

ALWAYS KNOW THE EXACT TIME WITHOUT A CLOCK

~OR~

BE ABLE TO DO MATH IN YOUR HEAD?

ALWAYS STINK AND NOT KNOW ABOUT IT

~OR~

ALWAYS SMELL SOMETHING THAT STINKS THAT NO
ONE ELSE NOTICES?

HAVE A SMALL PEBBLE STUCK IN YOUR SHOES

~OR~

A PERMANENT SPLINTER IN YOUR FINGER?

ALWAYS HAVE A MELODY STUCK IN YOUR HEAD

~OR~

HAVE THE SAME DREAM EVERY NIGHT FOR THE REST OF YOUR LIFE?

WOULD YOU RATHER...

HEAR THE BAD NEWS

~OR~

THE GOOD NEWS FIRST?

KNOW HOW TO PLAY EVERY INSTRUMENT

~OR~

KNOW EVERY LANGUAGE?

WOULD YOU RATHER...

HAVE TO DRESS ALL IN BRIGHT PURPLE

~OR~

ALL IN NEON GREEN FOR THE REST OF YOUR LIFE?

CLIMB A MOUNTAIN TO GET TO WORK(SCHOOL) EVERY DAY

~OR~

SWIM ACROSS A RIVER TO GET TO WORK(SCHOOL) EVERY DAY?

WOULD YOU RATHER...

WATCH ONE MOVIE FOR THE REST OF YOUR LIFE

~OR~

LISTEN TO ONE SONG FOR THE REST OF YOUR LIFE?

HAVE THE NECK OF A GIRAFFE

~OR~

THE EARS OF AN ELEPHANT?

WOULD YOU RATH-R...

PLAY YOUR FAVORITE VIDEO GAME

~OR~

WATCH YOUR FAVORITE MOVIE?

SNEEZE EVERY TIME YOU YAWN

~OR~

GET THE HICCUPS EVERY TIME YOU COUGH?

NEVER HAVE A NIGHTMARE AGAIN

~OR~

NEVER GET THE FLU EVER AGAIN?

HAVE YOUR OWN PLANE

~OR~

YOUR OWN HOT AIR BALLOON?

WOULD YOU RATHER...

SPEND A WEEK IN THE JUNGLE

~OR~

ONE NIGHT IN A HAUNTED HOUSE?

TAKE ONE PILL EVERY DAY TO FEEL FULL, AND NEVER EAT ANYTHING AGAIN

~OR~

EAT WHATEVER YOU WANT BUT ALWAYS FEEL HUNGRY?

NOT BE ABLE TO USE YOUR HANDS

~OR~

NOT BE ABLE TO WALK?

DRINK A GLASS OF MUDDY WATER

~OR~

EAT A CUP OF LAWN CLIPPINGS?

WOULD YOU RATHER...

NEVER BE ABLE TO USE A PLATE

~OR~

NEVER BE ABLE TO USE A FORK?

WASH YOUR HAIR WITH BAR SOAP

~OR~

WASH YOUR BODY WITH A HAND SANITIZER?

WOULD YOU RATHER...

TRAVEL FOR 5 YEARS IN AN RV

~OR~

TRAVEL FOR 5 YEARS ON A SAILBOAT?

HAVE NO KNUCKLES

~OR~

NO ELBOWS?

WOULD YOU RATHER...

ALWAYS FEEL SLEEPY DURING THE DAY

~OR~

ALWAYS HAVE INSOMNIA AT NIGHT?

NEVER GET A PAPER CUT AGAIN

~OR~

NEVER BITE YOUR TONGUE AGAIN?

BE ABLE TO READ VERY FAST

~OR~

BE ABLE TO WRITE/TYPE REALLY FAST?

BE ABLE TO SEE THROUGH WALLS

~OR~

BE ABLE TO HEAR SOUNDS FROM A MILE AWAY?

WOULD YOU RATHER...

DRINK AN ENTIRE GLASS OF SOY SAUCE

~OR~

EAT AN ENTIRE GLASS OF WASABI?

PASS EVERY TEST YOU TOOK WITHOUT STUDYING

~OR~

WIN EVERY SPORTS GAME YOU'VE EVER PLAYED?

HAVE A PIG NOSE

~OR~

A MONKEY TAIL?

BE A VEGAN

~OR~

ONLY BE ABLE TO EAT MEAT?

WOULD YOU RATH-R....

EAT ONE SMALL SPIDER

~OR~

HAVE 50 SMALL SPIDERS CRAWL ON YOU ALL AT ONCE?

BE COMPELLED TO HUG EVERYONE YOU MEET

~OR~

BE COMPELLED TO GIVE WEDGIES TO ANYONE IN A RED SHIRT?

BE A COWBOY WHO RIDES THE BULL

~OR~

RODEO CLOWN WHO DISTRACTS THE BULL?

HAVE EYES THAT CHANGE COLOR DEPENDING ON THE WEATHER

~OR~

HAIR THAT CHANGES COLOR DEPENDING ON YOUR MOOD?

EAT AN EGG WITH A HALF-FORMED CHICKEN INSIDE

~OR~

EAT FIVE BAKED CATERPILLARS?

BE UNABLE TO MOVE EVERY TIME IT RAINS

~OR~

NOT BE ABLE TO STOP MOVING WHEN IT'S SNOWING?

WOULD YOU RATHER...

NEVER HAVE ANOTHER EMBARRASSING FALL IN PUBLIC

~OR~

NEVER FEEL THE NEED TO FART IN PUBLIC?

FIGHT 100 CHICKEN-SIZED KANGAROO

~OR~

1 KANGAROO-SIZED CHICKEN?

WOULD YOU RATH-R...

YOUR ONLY MEANS OF TRANSPORTATION BE A CAMEL

~OR~

AN ELEPHANT?

ONLY BE ABLE TO EAT FROM A DOG BOWL

~OR~

ONLY BE ABLE TO DRINK FROM A SHOE?

NEVER HAVE TO EAT

~OR~

NEVER HAVE TO SLEEP?

LIVE THE NEXT 10 YEARS OF YOUR LIFE IN CHINA

~OR~

IN RUSSIA?

WOULD YOU RATH-R...

WATCH A MOVIE WITH NO SOUND

~OR~

LISTEN TO A MOVIE WITH NO VIDEO?

BE FORCED TO EAT ONLY SPICY FOOD

~OR~

ONLY TASTELESS BLAND FOOD?

WOULD YOU RATHER...

LIVE IN A VAULT

~OR~

LIVE IN A LIGHTHOUSE?

BE A GIANT TREE

~OR~

HAVE TO LIVE INSIDE A TREE FOR THE REST OF YOUR LIFE?

WOULD YOU RATHER...

ONLY LISTEN TO JAZZ MUSIC

~OR~

ONLY WATCH SILENT BLACK AND WHITE FILMS?

TAKE A SHOWER IN A PUBLIC PLACE EVERY DAY

~OR~

NEVER TAKE A SHOWER AT ALL?

WOULD YOU RATHER...

NEVER REMEMBER SOMEONE'S NAME

~OR~

NEVER REMEMBER SOMEONE'S FACE?

LIVE WITH SOMEONE WHO IS SLEEP-TALKING EVERY NIGHT

~OR~

SOMEONE WHO IS SNORING EVERY NIGHT?

WOULD YOU RATHER...

HAVE TO CLEAN THE TOILET ONCE A WEEK

~OR~

CLEAN THE GARBAGE CAN EVERY DAY?

HAVE NO EYELASHES

~OR~

ONLY ONE EYEBROW?

HAVE TO WEAR EVERY SHIRT INSIDE OUT

~OR~

ALWAYS WEAR DIFFERENT COLORED SHOES?

BE THE BEST PLAYER ON A LOSING BASKETBALL TEAM

~OR~

RIDE THE BENCH ON A WINNING TEAM?

DRINK ONLY WATER

~OR~

GIVE UP EATING PIZZA?

HAVE AN ACTUAL ROBOT

~OR~

AN ACTUAL SPACESHIP?

WOULD YOU RATHER...

NOT BE ABLE TO TASTE ANYTHING

~OR~

HAVE MILD BUT CONSTANT RINGING IN YOUR EARS?

HAVE ALL CATS TRY TO ATTACK YOU WHEN THEY SEE YOU

~OR~

ALL CROWS TRY TO ATTACK YOU WHEN THEY SEE YOU?

BE ABLE TO TASTE COLORS

~OR~

SMELL SOUNDS?

ALWAYS FEEL DIZZY

~OR~

ALWAYS HAVE A RUNNY NOSE?

BE ABLE TO RUN AS FAST AS A LION

~OR~

FLY, BUT ONLY AS FAST AS A TURTLE?

HAVE THE SAME PHONE FOREVER

~OR~

WEAR THE SAME CLOTHES FOR A YEAR?

LOSE YOUR SENSE OF SMELL

~OR~

YOUR SENSE OF TASTE?

BE ABLE TO BREATHE UNDERWATER

~OR~

FLY UP IN THE SKY?

WOULD YOU RATHER...

HAVE WINGS BUT YOU CAN'T FLY

~OR~

HAVE GILLS BUT YOU CAN'T BREATHE UNDERWATER?

HAVE BREAKFAST ON THE EIFFEL TOWER

~OR~

DINNER IN THE COLISEUM?

WOULD YOU RATHER...

ACCIDENTALLY STEP ON BROKEN GLASS

~OR~

ACCIDENTALLY STEP ON HOT COALS?

HAVE A CONDITION THAT MADE YOU FART 500 TIMES A DAY

~OR~

A CONDITION THAT MADE YOU PEE YOUR PANTS IN PUBLIC ONCE A YEAR?

WOULD YOU RATHER...

BE A PERSON THAT EVERYBODY STARING AT

~OR~

A PERSON THAT NO ONE NOTICES?

HAVE A PET UNICORN

~OR~

A PET DRAGON?

THE WORLD BE TAKEN OVER BY COMPUTERS

~OR~

BY ALIENS?

HAVE A BOTTOMLESS BOX OF LEGOS

~OR~

A BOTTOMLESS ICE CREAM BOX?

BE ABLE TO MAKE ANY IMAGINARY THING REAL BY JUST DRAWING IT

~OR~

MAKE ANY REAL THING DISAPPEAR BY TAKING ITS PHOTO?

BE FORCED TO SING ALONG EVERY TIME YOU HEAR A SONG

~OR~

BE FORCED TO DANCE EVERY TIME YOU HEAR MUSIC?

HAVE A BUCKET ON YOUR HEAD

~OR~

A CEMENT BLOCK ON YOUR FOOT?

HAVE REALLY SMALL HANDS

~OR~

REALLY BIG FEET?

LIVE IN A ROOM THAT'S BRIGHTLY LIT FOR AN ENTIRE MONTH

~OR~

LIVE IN A ROOM THAT'S KEPT PITCH BLACK FOR AN ENTIRE WEEK?

BECOME FIVE YEARS OLDER

~OR~

TWO YEARS YOUNGER?

HAVE TO DRINK ONLY HOT DRINKS ALL SUMMER LONG

~OR~

EAT ONLY COLD FOODS ALL WINTER LONG?

BE ABLE TO GO TO ANY DISNEYLAND FOR FREE FOR THE REST OF YOUR LIFE

~OR~

EAT FOR FREE AT ANY FAST FOOD RESTAURANT FOR THE REST OF YOUR LIFE?

WOULD YOU RATHER...

ALWAYS FEEL THAT SOMEONE IS FOLLOWING YOU BUT NO ONE REALLY IS

~OR~

ACTUALLY HAVE SOMEONE COMPLETELY HARMLESS FOLLOWING YOU?

HAVE A PERMANENT SPLINTER IN YOUR THUMB

~OR~

CHAPPED LIPS THAT NEVER HEAL?

BE ABLE TO GO BACK IN TIME

~OR~

TO FREEZE TIME WHENEVER YOU WANT?

HAVE A SMALL ROLE IN A GREAT MOVIE

~OR~

HAVE A BIG ROLE IN A BAD ONE?

WOULD YOU RATHER...

EAT A RAW POTATO

~OR~

A WHOLE LEMON?

HAVE A FLYING SKATEBOARD

~OR~

A CAR THAT CAN DRIVE UNDERWATER?

SLEEP IN YOUR CLOTHES

~OR~

SLEEP WITHOUT ANY BLANKETS OR PILLOWS?

EAT A BOWL OF ROTTEN EGGS

~OR~

RUN TWENTY LAPS AROUND THE BLOCK IN A PINK DRESS?

WOULD YOU RATHER...

30 HONEYBEES APPEAR OUT OF NOWHERE EVERY TIME YOU COUGH

~OR~

100 BUTTERFLIES DIE SOMEWHERE IN THE WORLD EVERY TIME YOU SNEEZE?

BE THE BEST AT SOMETHING THAT NO ONE TAKES SERIOUSLY

~OR~

BE MEDIOCRE AT SOMETHING WELL RESPECTED?

HAVE 3 LEGS

~OR~

3 HANDS?

HAVE A HEAD THE SIZE OF AN ORANGE

~OR~

THE SIZE OF A PUMPKIN?

BE ABLE TO FIND ANY LOST ITEM

~OR~

EVERY TIME YOU TOUCHED SOMEONE THEY WOULD BE UNABLE TO LIE?

BE ABLE TO REMEMBER EVERYTHING YOU'VE EVER HEARD

~OR~

BE ABLE TO PERFECTLY MIMIC ANY VOICE?

HAVE 5 SISTERS

~OR~

5 BROTHERS?

MOO LIKE A COW AFTER EVERY SENTENCE

~OR~

MEOW LIKE A CAT?

WOULD YOU RATHER...

HAVE A FAKE TAN ON YOUR FACE THAT'S TOO
BROWN

~OR~

TOO YELLOW?

REPLACE YOUR ARM WITH A HAMMER

~OR~

REPLACE YOUR LEG WITH A HOCKEY STICK?

WOULD YOU RATH-R...

HAVE MANY GOOD FRIENDS

~OR~

ONE VERY BEST FRIEND?

BE ABLE TO TURN THE LIGHTS ON WITH YOUR MIND

~OR~

BE ABLE TO TURN ANY CARPET ON THE FLOOR INTO
A FIVE-FOOT DEEP POOL OF WATER?

HAVE DONE SOMETHING EMBARRASSING AND ONLY YOUR FRIEND KNOWS ABOUT IT

~OR~

NOT DONE ANYTHING EMBARRASSING BUT EVERYONE EXCEPT YOUR FRIEND THINKS YOU DID IT?

BE ABLE TO READ TEN LANGUAGES BUT NOT BE ABLE TO SPEAK IN ANY OF THEM

~OR~

SPEAK TEN LANGUAGES BUT NOT BE ABLE TO READ?

YOUR REVIEW

I HOPE YOU'VE ENJOYED READING THIS LITTLE BOOK. AND IT WOULD BE GREAT IF YOU COULD TAKE A MOMENT OF YOUR TIME TO WRITE DOWN A SHORT REVIEW ON THE BOOK'S AMAZON PAGE. YOUR FEEDBACK IS VERY IMPORTANT TO ME. IT WILL ALSO HELP OTHERS TO MAKE AN INFORMED DECISION BEFORE PURCHASING THIS BOOK. THANK YOU IN ADVANCE,

- DAN GILDEN